GW00361298

Angel Messages

The Complete Book of Celestial Answers to Your Every Question

Juan Nakamori

Translated by
Akiko Fujinami

RIDER
LONDON · SYDNEY · AUCKLAND · JOHANNESBURG

3 5 7 9 10 8 6 4

This edition first published in 2004 by Rider, an imprint of Ebury Press, Random House,
20 Vauxhall Bridge Road, London SW1V 2SA

Random House Australia (Pty) Limited
20 Alfred Street, Milsons Point, Sydney, New South Wales 2061, Australia

Random House New Zealand Limited
18 Poland Road, Glenfield, Auckland 10, New Zealand

Random House (Pty) Limited
Isle of Houghton, Corner of Boundary Road and Carse O'Gowrie,
Houghton 2198, South Africa

The Random House Group Limited Reg. No. 954009

Papers used by Rider are natural, recyclable products made from wood grown
in sustainable forests.

Printed and bound in Great Britain by Mackays of Chatham plc, Kent

A CIP catalogue record for this book is available from the British Library

ISBN 9781844135561 (from January 2007)
ISBN 184413556X

How to Awaken Your Inner Angel

1. Hold the closed book, shut your eyes
and become aware of your breathing.

2. Gradually calm your thoughts and,
as you relax, focus on your question
or problem.

3. Send your question out into the
universe and wait.

4. Whichever number between 1 and 174
first comes to you, open that page
and study the message on it.
This is your answer.

You are born with love.

You are blessed to live

with love.

Nothing happens by coincidence. Every single event is designed to guide you towards inner awakening and true happiness.

3

Be as open hearted

as an innocent child.

Your potential will infinitely

increase.

4

Trust that whatever you truly need will be given to you at the right moment. Believe in this Universal Law and enjoy every aspect of your endeavour.

 5

Remember that you

create your own reality.

Whatever you do, create harmony

in yourself first.

You may choose to judge things

as right or wrong, and as superior

or inferior. But the Universe

accepts all matters as they are,

for what they are.

7

Focus on the challenge in hand.

As you sincerely and diligently

carry out your task, it will change

in the process.

Be confident, and love and

nourish yourself. You are gifted

with all the ability, charm and

energy you need.

 9

Gentleness heals and

strengthens your body and mind.

Gentleness embraces and

rejuvenates the bodies and minds

of those around you.

Consider each matter

with clarity and insight.

Let light and radiance flow

through your thoughts.

Will you diminish yourself

by competing and comparing

yourself with others?

Or will you increase your joy

by praising them?

Stop thinking for a while

and allow yourself to feel.

Your feelings will reveal much

more than thoughts alone

could explain.

———∞∞∞———

Be grateful for every single thing,

for every person and for all

of existence. Your heart-felt

gratitude will create a pathway

towards happiness.

🍃 **14** 🍃

As long as you continue

to blame others, the truth will

never be revealed to you.

When you calmly observe yourself,

you will awaken to reality.

───〜∞〜───

❦ 15 ❦

Trust in the divine nature
of your Inner Self. Free yourself
from your self-imposed
restrictions and consider your
infinite potential in life.

⸺❦⸺

Tidy up your surroundings and try to live simply. Your problems will gradually disappear with the clutter, allowing you to journey unburdened through life.

 17

As you free yourself from attachment, you will be freed from pain. Believe in your potential and rise to the challenge to change.

꩜

Take part in activities that

interest you, that you enjoy

and in which you can immerse

yourself. Enjoying yourself in this

way will water the flower

of your soul.

———❋❋———

Life is the eternal flow of 'Now'.

Feel the essence of Now

and live in the Now.

———∞∞∞———

Try to have a closer relationship

with yourself than with anyone

else. Real love means learning

to cherish your own thoughts

and feelings.

The Universe yearns to bless you
with innumerable gifts. It is only
waiting for you to open your
heart to receive them.

Every person is free to choose.

You yourself choose whether

to experience joy or pain,

to be happy or unhappy.

Enjoy visualising how you would

like your life to be. The more vivid

your dream, the greater the

chance of its coming true.

 24

To blame others

is to blame yourself.

To blame yourself is to

blame others.

━━━◦◦◦◦◦━━━

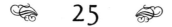

Self-righteousness and prejudice

will not afford you real insight

into the matter. Open your mind

and be brave enough to

communicate.

True love means giving without

demands or expectations. True

love means accepting without

judgement or restraint.

Take a good long look

at something that may

seem small and insignificant.

Therein lies a big message.

Each and every emotion offers

lessons to help you get to know

your Inner Self.

Do not reject or detest your

emotions, but accept and

experience them fully.

Allow the Universe to love you,

to guide you and to support you.

Always keep the door of your

heart wide open.

You are not expected to suffer

any hardship that you cannot

overcome. Instead of attempting

to escape from your problems,

accept them calmly and try to

resolve them.

᠁

Do not waste your energy

on that which is unworthy of you.

Live fully in this precious moment

with joy.

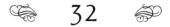

Be as free as the wind

and yet as strong as a mountain!

Expand your horizons as infinitely

as the sky, with the playfulness

of a bird!

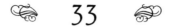 33

Your reality is a mirror

that reflects your Inner Self.

Observe it carefully and discover

yourself.

As you free yourself

from attachment, you will gain

spontaneity. As you remove

restrictions, you will gain freedom.

Relax and tune into the

harmonious rhythms of Nature.

Impatience and aggressive action

may well cause stagnation.

Treasure animals and plants.

Love them in the same way that

you love your friends.

It is often easy to blame,

but difficult to forgive.

And yet, although it may be hard,

forgiveness is surely always

worth trying.

38

Imagination is a seed of creation

that blooms like a flower.

Visualise a detailed picture of

the flower that you would like

to bloom.

Whatever it is, try to accept it

with a 'Thank you!' That way,

it will become yet one more

of life's blessings!

———∞∞∞———

Birds fly in the sky without worry and flowers bloom without fear. Nature is a treasure trove of such good examples, offering lessons for us all.

41

Live with enduring trust and
hope. Your Angel will always light
your way.

42

If you would like a significant wish to come true, start with several smaller wishes first. If you have plans and dreams for the future, begin by treasuring today.

You are born with so much

potential. But, if you say

to yourself, 'This is all I have',

indeed this is all you have.

Every person has inner goodness

and beauty. Every event holds

a valuable lesson and a beautiful

experience within it.

Instead of sticking to your

opinions stubbornly, open your

mind gracefully. As your thoughts

change, your situation will also

change.

 46

Cheer up others with your

wit and charm. Encourage them

with kind words.

———∞∞∞———

Release tension from your body

and mind, and relax. Take a deep

breath and communicate with

your Inner Light.

Accept small problems with

a smile and allow them to

fade away. Remain open minded

in order to accomplish

large tasks.

Will you stay where you are now, fearful of losing your security and comfort? Or, wishing to make true progress, will you take a brave step forward?

Offer your heart-felt gratitude

to the invisible Source of love and

guidance. You will always receive

help from this unseen power.

Accept all your emotions

consciously, without being swayed

by them. Taste each emotion fully,

but without over-indulging

yourself.

Everything that you send out

into the world will come back to

you. For you yourself create your

own signs in order that you might

begin to know yourself.

———❦———

If there is a problem, face it calmly. Rather than seeking a hasty solution, consider your situation objectively.

There are so many different paths
that you could follow. You just
have to choose the one that's
right for you, take a step forward
and then keep walking.

 55

If you have been grasping

onto something, try to let it go.

Your empty hands will be ready

to receive a new gift.

Do not complicate matters

by thinking too much about them.

The truth is really very simple.

Be as beautiful as a flower

in a field. Be as joyous as a bird

flying in the sky.

———◦∞∞◦———

Do not worry about what others
think of you. People will always
believe whatever they want.

———∞∞∞———

Everyone lives life

in his or her unique way.

Live your life honouring your

own unique way.

———— ∞∞∞ ————

60

Be gentle towards all living

things. Every single life is your

companion, your friend and

your teacher.

———∞∞∞———

Always keep your body, mind

and soul open. Angelic guidance

will come to you in the form

of your intuition.

Do not be weighed down

by past failures, blunders or errors.

For it is these experiences that will

lead you towards the opportunity

to achieve your goal.

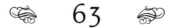 63

Everyone is born with a unique

personality and a mission in life.

Yours will flourish if you use

your positive characteristics

and your talents.

Try not to be affected by the

words and attitudes of others.

Instead, calmly consider your own

words and attitudes.

65

Set your priorities according

to the importance and urgency

of whatever faces you.

Do not neglect what you

must do now.

Enjoy, appreciate and learn from

the diversity of the four seasons.

likewise, enjoy and appreciate

every phase of your own life,

savouring its richness.

———∞∞∞———

❦   67   ❦

Happiness will never

come to you from the outside.

Not unless you open wide

the door of your heart.

———❦———

68

Be brave enough to do what

you really want to do.

Do whatever you enjoy with

enough conviction and you

will find success.

69

As you look up at the sky,

be aware of the blanket of

benevolence spread above you.

As you gently close your eyes,

know that blessings are raining

down upon you.

 70

Carefully observe the minor

details of your life. In your daily

life lies every seed necessary

for your spiritual growth.

———⟨⟨⟨⟩⟩⟩———

Open your mind and try to

face that person. Calm your mind

and try to talk to yourself.

Your tenderness is the warmth

of a spring sun. Your tenderness

is the fragrance of a flower

blooming in the desert.

 73

Think about what you

are holding on to. Therein lies

the root of your problems

and pain.

———⧇———

Inspiration is a gift from the

Source of love. Do not dam its

flow with thoughts and

judgements.

———————

Be generous and open-minded
when considering the business
of others. Be meticulous about
your own affairs and consider
them carefully.

 76

Observe every aspect

of the world. In doing so,

you will discover every aspect

of yourself.

Love forgives everything,

including failure, error, betrayal

and hatred. Love heals everything,

including discomfort, fear, pain

and loneliness.

Flowers are the stars of the earth

and birds are earth's Angels.

Every single life is a manifestation

of great love.

Being dedicated to someone

close to you is the same as being

dedicated to yourself. Serving a

stranger is the same as serving

the great Universe.

The source of every emotion

resides within you. No other

person is able to force emotions

upon you.

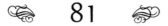

Say 'Thank you' promptly

and open-heartedly.

Enjoy the warmth of love

offered to you.

Offer your sincere gratitude

to your ancestors, parents and

family. Gratitude to those close

to you is a good starting point

on the road to happiness.

Life is studded with

innumerable opportunities.

There is no one who is not blessed

with these gifts.

A mind that asks for the moon

creates dissatisfaction and pain.

A mind that cherishes what it

already has invites fulfilment

and blessings.

 85

Flowing water is free of

stagnation, remaining fresh.

Drifting clouds are free of

attachment, remaining at liberty.

Your mission in life changes

according to the level of your

inner growth. Your current

mission is to do as much as you

are capable of doing now.

Asking without giving invites dissatisfaction. Giving without asking leads to contentment.

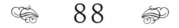

Trust all to the Universal laws

and to your own infinite

potential. The ultimate outcome

will always be for the Highest

Good.

89

Regardless of any excuses you make, you can never deceive yourself. Be brave and listen to your Inner Voice.

Many things are destined
to fade away, to decay or to
disappear. Seek eternal things
that never fade away
or disappear.

Do not fret about minor

conflicts or mistakes.

The important thing is to allow

yourself to be as useful as possible

in the circumstances.

Live your life honestly and

energetically. Never subjugate

yourself to the will of others

against your better judgement

and never live dishonestly.

 93

Wisdom and ability

flourish through acts of love.

Fill your thoughts, actions and

words with love.

———∞∞∞———

 **94**

Live simply and humbly. Live in

the awareness that there are many

things you just do not know

or understand.

———∞∞∞———

If you want to be powerful,

be spontaneous. Allow yourself

to merge, without pretension

or over-exertion, with the flow

of Nature.

Help will be granted to the soul
that seeks truth. New tasks and
blessings will be bestowed on the
soul that strives to make progress.

If you act with unwillingness
and from obligation, fatigue and
dissatisfaction will be your
harvest. If you act with hope
and enthusiasm, accomplishment
and growth will be your fruits.

———〜∞〜———

Treat yourself more gently.

Listen to that inner whisper urging

you to be gentle with yourself.

When you talk ceaselessly,

time flows away mercilessly.

When you listen calmly,

a wonderful awakening occurs.

Patience nourishes you with

confidence and compassion.

But, in order to receive these gifts,

patience must be combined

with willingness.

Jealousy and attachment do not

resonate with the vibration of the

Source of love. Understanding

and tolerance are at one

with the Source.

Absorb love and energy from

the sun into your body and mind.

Let tenderness and strength shine

into your daily life.

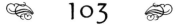 103

A mind that condemns

and criticises diminishes your

potential. A mind that is humble,

open and flexible increases

your capability.

Disappointment

is a common companion in life.

Your life will take shape according

to how you react to it.

———∞———

Everyone has his or her own

values, yet there is only one Truth.

That which we value reveals the

level of our spiritual growth.

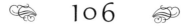

Accept yourself as you are now.

Accept others as they are now.

No one else is able to cause you

pain. Heal the cause of your pain

by embracing love.

Everyone has curious character

quirks. Try to view each person

as objectively and compassionately

as possible.

This is your only life and you

will never be able to repeat it.

Cherish and live each day of your

life fully, with delight.

Even amidst chaos and in times

of trouble, remain calm and

composed.

———∞∞∞———

Instead of angrily doling out blame, try to offer gentle encouragement. Do this regardless of whether you are dealing with yourself or others.

Do not regret what has
already been done. Pour your love
and strength into whatever
lies ahead of you.

Respect each glimmer of

intuition that sparks within you.

Treasure all the signs that your

Guardian Angel sends to you.

Get to know yourself properly
first. If you do not know yourself,
you will not be able to know
others or Divinity.

115

No matter what your

circumstances are, do not resist

them but befriend them.

No matter what a person is like,

do not reject him or her,

but pass on your love.

As long as you cannot forgive,

your pain will stay with you.

Uplift your mind, and

embrace all.

Remember, you were born

to be happy. Keep faith in this

and move on.

You are never alone.

The Creator's love is always

with you, deep within you.

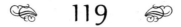 119

Confidence means trusting

completely in your own potential.

Freedom means loosening yourself

from your own restrictions.

You cannot grasp mere illusions

no matter how desperately you

visualise or crave for them.

You must visualise hope instead,

and face reality courageously.

You have already been given all that you need. As you begin to make proper and joyous use of this, you will receive even more.

Loss creates an opportunity

to receive many things. Within the

pain of loss lies all-encompassing

compassion.

By yourself, you could not create

a single hair or a single finger.

Your abilities are granted to you

by the love and power of the

Creator.

Instead of considering a matter
from your single viewpoint, try to
observe it from the perspective
of others. Instead of worrying only
about your own interests, consider
the well-being of the whole.

Negative thoughts attract

negative events. Positive thoughts

invite positive events.

Consider whether a particular

problem or pattern keeps

repeating itself in your life.

If it does, this is the voice of your

Inner Self, calling you again and

again to wake up.

Fate is not what governs you.

Fate is what you choose and

create for yourself.

128

You can only do as much as you

can do now. Trust the rest to the

wisdom of Nature.

Treasure every precious
encounter. To treasure your
relationships is to treasure
your life.

————⟨⟩————

Discover the brilliance within

yourself. In so doing, you will

unearth the brilliance in every

person you meet.

———❦———

131

Your thoughts, words and

actions will always return to you.

Like an echo, they will come back

to you straight away.

You have chosen your parents, brothers and sisters. You have chosen your fate, your destiny and your physical body.

Do not worry about the results
of all the efforts you have made.
Be grateful and happy with
yourself for having done
the best you can.

134

Do you spend your time

reminiscing about the past,

or worrying about the future?

Live truly and fully

in this moment.

────⊗⊗⊗────

Try not to withhold your

feelings for fear of getting hurt.

If you express them with love,

you will create an opportunity

for better understanding.

No matter how difficult your circumstances, never give up hope. Trust in the wisdom of the Creator as, out of the blue, events may turn in your favour.

Do not shy away from the dark

clouds of your mind, but accept

them and try to understand them.

They have appeared for

good reason.

Stop being so serious, and try
to be more cheerful and playful!
Stop being so strict, and try to be
more soft and gentle!

Create a space for pure and

earnest prayer. Your prayer will be

a stream of light, reaching to

where the Angels are.

Carefully cleanse your mind's

eye of clouds and impurities.

Then, goodness, beauty and

truthfulness will be revealed to

you.

Only through seeing yourself
reflected in others will you be
able to know yourself and grow.
Only through your relationships
with others will you be able to
improve yourself and live life fully.

Spare a moment in which

to relax. Use this moment's calm

to open yourself to flashes

of inspiration.

Do not worry about your age,

the depth of your knowledge or

the breadth of your experiences.

Celestial guidance comes to all

those who crave it.

 144

Free your mind from attachment

to limited plans and schemes.

As you do so, new ideas will come

to you from the great Source

of love.

Innocence is not only a gift for children. Innocence is to be even more treasured as you grow.

Spite, displeasure,

obtrusiveness and stubbornness.

These are all expressions of

minds that crave love.

You are a part of the entire

Universe. You are at one with

the entire Universe.

Do not be troubled even if you discover your baser instincts, but encourage them to follow the example of your Higher Self. In the school of life, the baser instincts are students and the Higher Self their teacher.

'Life' means acknowledging

this very moment. 'Love' means

living in this very moment.

Increase your courage and love,

and accept all. The Universal Law

is based in complete acceptance.

Do not worry about your past,

regardless of how hard it has

been. Start a new life right now

with fresh resolve.

If you act with uncertainty,

you will produce uncertain results.

If you act with confidence,

you will receive the support

of the Universe.

Even if things do not go quite as you would like them to, do not worry. In order to achieve a balance, carry on with joy and enthusiasm, anticipating the outcome with a peaceful mind.

 154

Embrace the warmth of the sun

with your entire body and soul.

Your body and soul will be filled

with light, strength and love.

Do not be afraid to reveal
yourself. You will be rewarded
with true freedom, like a naked
child swimming in the ocean.

Friendships form part of your

life, the essence of who you are –

your mind and your body.

To treasure your friends is to

treasure yourself.

 157

Close your eyes lightly

and breathe calmly.

Feel how loved you are.

As long as you choose to blame

others or your circumstances,

you will never find happiness.

For it is your soul that has chosen

to experience all these problems.

Great joy can be found even in

the tiniest thing that could fit

into the palm of your hand.

Sense it through the Inner Light

that resides deep within you.

 160

Forgive and love yourself

unconditionally.

Forgive and love every other

person unconditionally.

Do not be swayed by the

thoughts of others nor worry

about the opinion that others may

have of you. Believe in yourself

and stay true to yourself.

As you strive hard to master one

thing, you will spontaneously be

able to understand many others.

An enquiring mind provides wings

with which to soar freely.

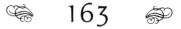 163

You do not need to grieve over

your inabilities or weaknesses.

Your mission in life is to display

your unique qualities and

strengths.

164

Within every situation,

brightness can be found.

Within every person,

Divinity shines.

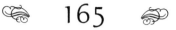 165

You are a child of the great

Source of love. You are blessed

to live in great love.

Uncertainty, fear, worry and hatred are illusions created by your mind. They will disappear through gratitude, trust, compassion and devotion.

 167

The Universal Law supports you
according to the needs of your
soul. Every event supports and
nourishes the growth of your soul.

168

Observe how you project

yourself onto every person and

every situation. Self-knowledge

opens the door to truth.

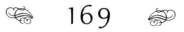

169

Your physical body will disappear

one day. Seek to know your soul,

which enjoys eternal life.

————◆◆◆————

Each and every moment brings
with it the opportunity to create
a new self. Live in this present
moment and be open minded.

Any negative can be changed to

a positive. The power to transform

negatives into positives is

inherently yours.

172

After a storm, the sun shines forth brightly – such is the wisdom of the Universe. After an ordeal, the soul shines forth brilliantly – such are the blessings of the Universe.

 173

Fill your thoughts with brightness

and serenity. Therein lies the key

to your spiritual progress.

You are protected this very

moment, always and forever.

Take comfort in this and live

your life in harmony with

your Higher Self.

EPILOGUE

As the title of this book suggests, I am not the true author of these messages, which came to me in sudden flashes of inspiration. When I received them, I had to stop thinking, empty myself and tune into the Universe. You could say that I received the messages as inner vibrations, which I then tried to express in words. Even though I do not practise any particular religion or follow one spiritual path, I feel truly grateful that I have been able to share this gift, which spontaneously appeared in my life, with you.

Our amazing Universe supports the existence of every creature on earth. Its nurturing care means that we are empowered and blessed with the elements and lessons necessary for our individual growth. In this respect, the message that you have chosen intuitively in this book may be one that your Higher Self wishes to send to you.

* * *

Juan Nakamori was born in Tokyo, Japan. Looking up at the sky one night, she had a vision of a multitude of angels filling the heavens. Since then, the angel messages that she has received have filled readers around the world with love and encouragement, offering them healing and enlightenment. She has published a number of best-selling books drawing upon this celestial wisdom.